Top Score Writing

Top Score Writing, Inc. © 2020

ISBN: 978-1-952519-13-0

By: Lisa Collum, M.Ed.

This comprehensive writing curriculum has been designed for third grade teachers to prepare their students for the state writing assessment. The curriculum will provide extensive instruction in informative, opinion, and narrative writing. This curriculum includes lessons, practice worksheets, quizzes, homework assignments, and practice writing tests.

The lessons were created to provide a simple approach to writing that is practical for ALL students. This writing foundation will assist your students in becoming great writers.

This curriculum is divided into six sections: Expository Writing, Informative Writing, Opinion Writing, Advanced Lessons, Narrative Writing, and Additional Activities and Strategies.

www.topscorewriting.com

Table of Contents

SECTION 3: Opinion Writing

SECTION 4: Advanced Lessons

Informative:

SECTION 5: Narrative Writing

SECTION 6: Additional Activities and Strategies

Top Score Writing

SECTION 5

Narrative Writing

WRITING: LESSON 74

Today will be the first day we introduce the narrative essay.
The students must be able to distinguish which prompts are expository, narrative, and opinion.
Therefore, we will begin the narrative teaching with an overview of prompts.

Review the 3 Types of Essays:
- Explain to students that there are three types of essays we have been working on: informative, opinion, and narrative.
- For the past few weeks, we have been working on only informative and opinion.
- Now we are moving on to narrative essays.
- The way you decide which type of essay to write is by looking at the keyword(s) in the prompt.
- *The prompts we have been doing have all had what word (s) in them?* **Explain, Inform, Opinion, Think/Feel**
- These are the keywords for an informative and opinion essay.
- *Does anyone remember what the keywords are for a narrative essay?* **Tell and Story**
- Hand out the worksheet titled "Example Prompts."
- *Let's look at some examples. Start with #1 and underline the keyword. What is the keyword?* **Informative**
- *So what type of essay is it?* **Informative.** *How do we plan for this type of essay?* **ITC**
- *Look at #2. What is the keyword?* **Story.** *What type of essay is this?* **Narrative.** *Do we use an IRC/ITC outline for this?* **No**
- *In a few minutes, I will be showing you how we plan for a narrative essay.*
- *Look at the third example, what is the keyword?* **Tell**
- *What type of essay is this?* **Narrative.** *Do we plan with an IRC outline?* **No**
- Look at the *last one. What is the keyword?* **Opinion**
- *What type of essay is this?* **Opinion.** *Do we plan with an IRC outline?* **Yes**

Planning for a Narrative Essay:
- To plan for a narrative essay, we use a BTE OUTLINE.
- The **B** stands for <u>Beginning</u>.
    T stands for <u>Things that happened</u>. (There are always 3 things that happen in a narrative.)
    E stands for <u>Ending</u>. (This is how the story ended.)
- It is like an IRC outline because you have a beginning, three things that happened, and an ending.
- Tell students that there will be no T, 3A, or 3B sentences. This is a totally different type of essay.
- When writing a narrative; you are telling a story. You do not explain anything. You do not have 3 reasons, you have *3 things that happen.*
- Now let's do an example.
- Here is the prompt: *(Write on the board.)*

Sometimes we get to go on vacation. Before you write, think about a time you went somewhere on vacation. Now write a story about the time you and your family went on a vacation.

Write this planning outline on the board:

B   _____
T1 _____
T2 _____
T3 _____
E   _____

Explain that the **B** stands for what happened at the **B**eginning of the story.

- **T1** stands for the first **T**hing that happened in your story.

- **T2** is the second **T**hing that happened in your story, and T3 is the third Thing that happened in your story.

- **E** stands for how the story **E**nded.

- Let's plan this one together. We'll start with how the story began. Let's say that we were at school working on writing and then all of a sudden there was an announcement for us to come to the office for dismissal. Then our family was waiting for us to go on vacation.

- So the beginning of the story is: we were at school, we got our things and headed to the office for dismissal. Next to B, write *Left School*. Remember, we want to keep our planning short. Instead of writing "We were at school, lined up, and got on the bus" we just write "Left School." Just put a quick summary/main idea of what happened on planning sheet. Save the details for your essay!

- How did our story begin? We left school and headed on vacation with our family!

- Then we go to T1 – the first thing that happened. How about we end up in Hawaii?

> T1 <u>Hawaii</u>

- Let's think about the second thing that happened. We just arrived in Hawaii. How about we go snorkeling?

The planning for T2 should look like this:

> T2 <u>Snorkeling</u>

Now for T3, let's say we went ziplining.

The planning for T3 should look like this:

T3 <u>Ziplining</u>

The "E" paragraph is how the story ends. We need to head back home and wrap up vacation.

• So E can be "Back Home" since we go back home in the ending paragraph.

The planning for E should look like this:

E <u>Back Home</u>

B   <u>Left School</u>
T1 <u>Hawaii</u>
T2 <u>Snorkeling</u>
T3 <u>Ziplining</u>
E   <u>Back Home</u>

• Hand out narrative "Student Practice/Homework" sheet.

• Allow students to finish for homework.

Example Prompts   Name:_____

1. Write an informative essay to present to your class about weather. Use information from the passages in your essay. *What type of essay is this? Narrative, Opinion, or Informative?*

2. Volunteering can be very rewarding. Before you begin writing, think about times when you have volunteered to help other people. Tell a story about a time when you volunteered. *What type of essay is this? Narrative, Opinion, or Informative?*

3. People dream of discovering treasure. Imagine that one day you discovered a treasure chest. Now tell about happened when you opened this treasure chest. *What type of essay is this? Narrative, Opinion, or Informative?*

4. Do you think students should be allowed to chew gum in school? Write an essay in which you give your opinion. *What type of essay is this? Narrative, Opinion, or Informative?*

Student Practice/Homework   Name:_____

Directions: Read the following prompt. Plan for the essay using the BTE outline.

Your birthday should be an enjoyable day! Imagine that you had one birthday that was more special than the others. Write a story about your special birthday.

B_____

T1_____

T2_____

T3_____

E_____

Everyone has a favorite celebrity. Think of one celebrity that you would love to meet. Write a story about the time you met your favorite celebrity.

B_____

T1_____

T2_____

T3_____

E_____

WRITING: LESSON 75

Today you will be working on planning for a narrative essay again.
You will do an example with the class, and then students will work on a plan of their own.

***Example Planning:

- Write this prompt on the board:

> *Magic keys usually can be seen on TV and in fantasy movies. Before you write,*
> *think about what you would do if you were to find a magic key.*
> *Now tell what happened after you discovered the magic key.*

- We want to make sure that the key does something interesting.
- For today's practice, we will find the key while walking home from school.
- Pass out the planning sheets.
- Let's start with the "B" paragraph. We are going to find a key. We have to find the key in the B paragraph and then write 3 things we did with the key in T1, T2, and T3.
- So for **B**eginning, **B**, write the following:

> B <u>Key</u>

- Now we need to talk about the first **T**hing that happened, "T1". How about we take the key and open up a secret door?

> T1 <u>Secret Door</u>

- The second **T**hing that happened, T2. Let's think about it. It needs to be interesting. How about we fall into an underground world?

> T2 <u>Underground World</u>

- Now the third **T**hing that happened, T3, is that we find the treasure chest that the key can open. So T3 should look like this:

> T3 <u>Treasure Chest</u>

- For the Ending, "E," the key needs to open the treasure chest and make us rich so we can take it home to our family. We can say that we quickly climbed a ladder out of the underground world which led us out and back into the room with the secret door.

E <u>Go Home</u>

***Student Practice:

- Now the students will practice on their own.
- During this time, walk around the room and make sure they are planning correctly.
- Write this prompt on the board:

   People dream of discovering gold. Imagine that one day while you were gardening, you dug up gold. Now tell a story about what you did with the gold once you found it.

- Brainstorm with students to give some ideas. They could take the gold and buy a mansion, or they could buy everyone in their school a ticket to Disney World! They have to somehow find the gold in B. Then they do three things with it (T1, T2, and T3).

- Give students 15 minutes to work on this.

Planning Sheet   Name:_____

B_____

T1_____

T2_____

T3_____

E_____

Student Practice/Homework   Name:_____

Directions: Read the following prompt. Plan for the essay using the BTE outline.

People dream of discovering gold. Imagine that one day while you were gardening, you dug up gold. Now tell a story about you did with the gold once you found it.

B_____

T1_____

T2_____

T3_____

E_____

WRITING: LESSON 76

Today the students will be learning how to write the "B" paragraph. Remember that the "B" paragraph stands for the "Beginning." This paragraph is how the whole story started.

- Do an example on the board:

Sometimes we get to go on vacation. Before you write, think about a time you went somewhere on vacation. Now write a story about the time you and your family went on a vacation.

- Review the prompt.
- Start planning. Make sure you do not spend more than ten minutes on planning. Today we want to focus on the "B" paragraph. This means you can ask the students for ideas, but move on quickly. You may have to plan most of it on your own.
- Here is the planning for this prompt:

   B   Left School
   T1 Hawaii
   T2 Snorkeling
   T3 Ziplining
   E   Back Home

- Now that you are done planning, you will write the "B" paragraph.
- Here are some key points to mention to the students:
   - ✓ The "B" paragraph tells how the story began.
   - ✓ You have to tell where you were (the setting).
   - ✓ Whatever has to happen, has to happen in the "B" paragraph. (*Ex. If you have to find a book, find it in the "B" paragraph.*)
- Show "Narrative Story Starters" sheet under the document camera.
- Go over the different ways to start a narrative essay.
- Tell students to pick 1 or 2 story starters and stick with them for all of their stories.
- So let's use our planning and write the "B" paragraph.
   - We know we were in school practicing writing. Suddenly an announcement came on over the loudspeaker, and it said that we needed to pack up for dismissal.

- Now let's write that in a descriptive paragraph.

   Let me tell you about the time my family and I went on a vacation to Hawaii. It all started two weeks ago in Mrs. Lee's class when we were working on writing our narrative essays. The clock struck 9:00 a.m., when a sudden announcement came on over the loudspeaker for me to pack up for dismissal. I was totally shocked and confused. It was still very early in the morning! I still had all day until I was supposed to go home! But I followed the directions and packed my bookbag to go home. As I was walking down the hallway towards the office, I could see my entire family screaming and waving at me to hurry up. We supposedly had a flight to catch to Hawaii!

- That is an example of a "B" paragraph. It is descriptive, provides lots of details, and tells exactly how the story began.
- Now students will start their homework. The homework is to plan for an essay and then write the "B" paragraph. Students *will not* write the whole essay. They will only plan and write the "B" paragraph.

Narrative Story Starters

- It all began
- It all started
- I remember it like it was yesterday
- Let me tell you about the
- Wait until you hear
- The day began with
- Once upon a time
- Did you ever think that
- The day started with

Describe the setting *(where you are, what it is like there)*

Example 1: Prompt about going to the movie theater
   - The theater was packed with rows of people chomping on popcorn and slurping sodas.

Example 2: Prompt about going to the beach
   - The sun was shining bright, and it was a perfect day to ride some waves and get a tan.

Example 3: Prompt about a sleepover
   - The sleeping bags were lined up next to each other, and the pizzas were on their way!

Example 4: Prompt about a scary moment
   - Rain was pouring down outside, and lightning was flashing in the distance.

Homework   Name:_____

For this practice, you are only planning and writing for the "B" paragraph. Read the prompt, plan for the "B" paragraph, and then write a "B" paragraph using the template.

1.) Everyone has a favorite celebrity. Think of one celebrity that you would love to meet. Write a story about the time you met your favorite celebrity.

B _____

Now write the "B" paragraph:

_____

_____

_____

_____

_____

_____

2.) Your birthday should be an enjoyable day! Imagine that you had one birthday that was more special than the others. Write a story about your special birthday.

B _____

Now write the "B" paragraph:

_____

_____

_____

_____

_____

_____

WRITING: LESSON 77

Today you will be reviewing the "B" paragraph. You will do one example together, and then students will do four on their own. In the next few lessons, we will start writing a narrative essay. So we want to make sure students can plan and write a good "B" paragraph today.

Prompt: Christmas is a time when memories are made. Think of one Christmas that was more special than others. Write a story about your time celebrating that Christmas.

- Let's think of a story about a Christmas we celebrated. This can be a real story, or we can make it all up! Let's make this one really interesting and make it up. We can write a story about a snowman we made that came to life!
- Remember, we should only spend about 15-20 minutes on planning.

    Example Planning:
    B Christmas Eve
    T1 Snowman
    T2 Christmas Caroling
    T3 Snowball Fight
    E Disappeared/Ornament

- Now, let's write a really good "B" paragraph for this story. We want to tell how the whole story started.

Example "B" Paragraph:

      Let me tell you about a Christmas I will never forget. It all started on Christmas Eve night. A huge blizzard was taking place outside. The snow was piling up on the streets and homes in our neighborhood. After church and dinner, my siblings and I decided it was the most perfect night to go outside and play in the snow. Our parents agreed as they thought it would be a special way to spend Christmas Eve together. We decided we were going to build the biggest snowman ever. So, we got right to work rolling three large snowballs. My mom went inside to find a carrot for a nose, a scarf, and a hat to put on top of the snowman's head. When we stacked the snowballs on top of each other and placed the hat on his head, something strange happened! The snow started to whip around, and it got really bright. Immediately when it stopped, we heard a voice that said, "Merry Christmas." The snowman was talking to us!

- Now students are going to try some planning and "B" paragraphs on their own. Whatever is not finished in class, should be finished for homework. After this lesson, we will not be teaching narrative planning anymore. Next lesson we will work on writing the essays.
- Hand out the "Student Practice/ Homework" sheets.

Example Answer – Prompt 1:

      The day began with my mom yelling down the hallway, "Get up! You're going to be late for school!" I jumped out of bed and ran to the bathroom to do my typical bathroom routine of washing my face, brushing my teeth, and putting my hair up in a high ponytail. This morning was different though. When I looked in the mirror, instead of seeing me, I was seeing my best friend Lizzie! I realized that overnight, I had turned into her. Therefore, I think she must have turned into me! I quickly put on some sunglasses and a hat and ran out the door toward the bus stop. I had to figure out what was going on here!

Student Practice/Homework   Name:_____

For this assignment, you will plan and write the "B" paragraph for four different prompts.
You are NOT writing a full essay, only plan and write the "B" paragraph.
Make sure your "B" paragraph tells how the whole story started.

**Prompt 1: Sometimes we wish we lived the life of another person. Imagine that one day
you had the chance to switch lives with your best friend. Write a story about
the day that you switched lives with your best friend.**

Planning

B _____

T1 _____

T2 _____

T3 _____

E _____

"B" paragraph

_____

_____

_____

_____

_____

_____

_____

_____

Name:_____

Prompt 2: Many children love to play video games.
Imagine you were playing a video game and got sucked into it.
Now tell what happened when you got sucked into the video game.

Planning

B _____

T1 _____

T2 _____

T3 _____

E _____

"B" paragraph

_____

_____

_____

_____

_____

_____

_____

_____

Name:_____

Prompt 3: Some people rescue animals as part of their jobs, and others do it as an act of kindness. Imagine that one day you became a hero by helping an animal in need. Now write a story about the day that you helped an animal.

Planning

B _____

T1 _____

T2 _____

T3 _____

E _____

"B" paragraph

_____

_____

_____

_____

_____

_____

_____

_____

Name:_____

Prompt 4: Everybody imagines having the perfect dream job.
Imagine for one day you got to do your dream job.
Write a story about that day.

Planning

B _____

T1 _____

T2 _____

T3 _____

E _____

"B" paragraph

_____

_____

_____

_____

_____

_____

_____

_____

WRITING: LESSON 78

Today the students will be concentrating on their three things that happened in their story (middle paragraphs). These three paragraphs are the most crucial for the students overall score. They have to be interesting, meaningful and include LOTS of details.

1.   Here is the prompt for today's lesson:

Sometimes we get to go on vacation. Before you write, think about a time you went somewhere on vacation. Now write a story about the time you and your family went on a vacation.

2.   Use the planning below for today's lesson.

   B   Left School
   T1 Hawaii
   T2 Snorkeling
   T3 Ziplining
   E   Back Home

3.   Review planning. (This is the story we have been working on.)

4.   Since planning is done, let's start writing.

   Please place 4 large post-it notes/chart paper on the board to model the next 4 paragraphs of this lesson.

5.   In the last few lessons, we worked on the "B" paragraph, so this should be easy.

6.   Here is the "B" paragraph we wrote for this prompt:

   Let me tell you about the time my family and I went on a vacation to Hawaii. It all started two weeks ago in Mrs. Lee's class when we were working on writing our narrative essays. The clock struck 9:00 a.m., when a sudden announcement came on over the loudspeaker for me to pack up for dismissal. I was totally shocked and confused. It was still very early in the morning! I still had all day until I was supposed to go home! But I followed the directions and packed my bookbag. As I was walking down the hallway toward the office, I could see my entire family screaming and waving at me to hurry up. We supposedly had a flight to catch to Hawaii!

7.   Now we will write about the first thing that happened in the story. Review planning and what should be included in each paragraph. (This paragraph should be about arriving in Hawaii.) Students need to include what they see, what they did, details about it, and how they feel. Their last sentence should move on to the next thing and lead the reader into the next paragraph. Ask for ideas from the class and then write the T1 paragraph. Here is an example of what this paragraph can look like:

   Before long, we arrived at the airport and boarded our plane. My parents had my suitcase all packed and ready, so I grabbed it and headed off to the terminal. We grabbed some snacks and magazines on the way, as it was going to be a long flight! We were taking a non-stop flight to Oahu, Hawaii, and it took about 12 hours to get there. On the plane ride, I asked my mom why she didn't tell me we were going on vacation. She said she wanted it to be a surprise for my good grades I was getting in school. I told her that I loved the surprise and was so excited to get there! After several movies, naps, and games with my siblings, we arrived in Hawaii!

8. Now you will write about the second thing that happened in this story. This is about going snorkeling. Here is an example of what it should look like:

   When we stepped out of the airport, it was hot and steamy. We could see lush mountains and tropical birds flying above. We grabbed a cab to our hotel and immediately got our bathing suits on. We all decided we wanted to go snorkeling. According to the man at the front desk of the hotel, there was a late afternoon snorkel trip going out at 4:00 p.m. It was perfect timing! We jumped on the boat and headed out to sea. We didn't have to go far off shore until we were allowed to get in the water. When I put my mask on and saw what was underneath me, I was in shock! There was the most magnificent ocean reef with many brightly colored fish swimming all around it. There were even Nurse Sharks lying against the sand on the bottom! It was so beautiful! I swam for hours not wanting to ever get out! When it started to get dark though, our captain said it was time to go back to shore. When I got out of the water and dried off, I realized how amazing that experience was!

9. Now it is time to write about the third thing that happened in this story. This paragraph is all about going ziplining. Here is an example of what you can write:

   After many days of relaxing and playing on the beach, we had our next fun adventure. It was the last day of the trip, and we wanted to make it the best day! We decided to do something crazy and go ziplining! We had to hike up a large mountain in the rainforest to get to the ziplining site. It was drizzling, and it was hard work getting to the top. Once we were there though, it was all worth it! I got harnessed in, and I was pushed off the side of a ledge where I went zipping through the air like a monkey. As I was flying from tree to tree, I could see plenty of tropical plants, insects, and creatures! Although the ziplining cord was miles long, it only lasted a few minutes. I wished it was longer because it was the best time of my life!

10. Today we are not going to write the "E" paragraph. Explain to the students that the ending of the story is about going back home. It should tell all about how the whole trip ended and how it was time to go home.

11. Now the students will work on their homework. Hand out the "Homework" sheet and let them begin working on their essay. Walk around and make sure they are planning correctly. If there are students who are still struggling with planning, pull them aside and work with them in small group.

Homework   Name:_____

Many children love to play video games. Imagine you were playing a video game and got sucked into it. Now tell what happened when you got sucked into the video game.

B_____

T1_____

T2_____

T3_____

E_____

B
_____
_____
_____
_____

T1
_____
_____
_____
_____
_____
_____
_____
_____

T2
_____
_____
_____
_____
_____
_____
_____
_____

T3

_____

_____

_____

_____

_____

_____

_____

_____

_____

E

_____

_____

_____

_____

WRITING: LESSON 79

Today you will be teaching the "E" paragraph. You will use yesterday's planning and the 4 paragraphs you wrote as a class. Pull those out and hang them across the board. Take one more large post-it note/chart paper and place it on the end. This is where you will write the "E" paragraph.

1. The "E" paragraph is 4-6 sentences. You want to make sure you include the following:
   - How you got back, changed back, or how something stopped working.
   - What you did when you got back or returned.
   - Feeling you had about the day.

2. Take ideas from the class.

3. Write the "E" paragraph together.

4. Here is an example of what it can look like:

   That night after ziplining, I was thinking about how incredible my vacation was with my family. We all had the most amazing time and got to see things we had never seen before. I felt very thankful and lucky to have such a great experience. Very quickly, I fell asleep and was woken up at 2:00 a.m. to catch our flight back home. Although it was a long journey to get there, it was all worth it! It was the best surprise ever!

5. Hand out "Student Practice" sheet.

6. Give quiz.

Student Practice   Name:_____

"E" Paragraph Practice

For this practice worksheet, you are only planning and writing for the "E" paragraph.
Read the prompt, plan for the "E" paragraph, and then write the "E" paragraph.

***Christmas is a time when memories are made. Think of one Christmas that was
more special than others. Write a story about your time celebrating that Christmas.***

B Christmas Eve
T1 Snowman
T2 Christmas Caroling
T3 Snowball Fight
E Disappeared/Ornament

**This story is about how the snowman you made comes to life on Christmas Eve. You go
Christmas caroling and have a snow ball fight with him. The end of the story is you going to bed
that night and waking up in the morning to find he has disappeared. When you go downstairs
to open presents, you notice a new ornament on the tree. It's a snowman! Write the ending of the
story.*

Now write the E Paragraph:

_____

_____

_____

_____

_____

_____

Quiz   Name:_____

"E" Paragraph – Quiz

For this quiz, you are only planning and writing for the "E" paragraph.
Read the prompt, plan for the "E" paragraph, and then write the "E" paragraph.

Your birthday should be an enjoyable day! Imagine that you had one birthday that was more special than the others. Write a story about your special birthday.

B Wake Up
T1 Birthday Party
T2 Taylor Swift
T3 Sings
E Guitar

This story is about how you wake up and you go to your birthday party. Taylor Swift ends up coming to your party as a surprise. She hangs out with you and your friends and sings happy birthday to you. At the end of the story, before she leaves, she signs her guitar and gives it to you as a gift. Write the ending of the story.

Now write the E Paragraph:

_____

_____

_____

_____

_____

_____

WRITING: LESSON 80

Today we are going to practice writing a story together.
For this lesson, it is best if you have 6 big post-it notes/chart paper to put across the board.
One for planning and five for the paragraphs.

Prompt: Magic keys usually can be seen on TV shows and in fantasy movies.
Before you write, think about what would happen if you were to find a magic key.
Now tell what happened after you discovered a magic key.

1. Let's Plan! What HAS to happen in B? We have to find the magic key.

2. Have students generate ideas. Let's pretend we were walking home and found a magical key.

B – Key

3. Now let's think about 3 things that happened. What if you really found a magical key? What would you do? We want our 3 things to be exciting.

4. Let students generate/share ideas.

5. Let's make this interesting. How about the magical key opens a secret door in the attic of our house?

T1 – Secret Door

6. Now if we go to different places in our middle paragraphs using our key, we have to somehow get back home in the ending paragraph!

T2 – Underground World (In this paragraph, you will fall into an underground world.)

T3 – Treasure Chest (In this paragraph, you find a treasure chest that the magic key can open.)

E – Go Home

So our planning looks like this:
B   Key
T1 Secret Door
T2 Underground World
T3 Treasure Chest
E   Go Home

7. Let's start with the "B" paragraph. Remember your story starters!
    Example: It all started one ordinary Wednesday when I was walking home from school.

8. Now tell how it all started.
    Example: I was listening to music on my iPhone, texting my best friend about soccer practice when I stumbled upon a glowing key in the middle of the sidewalk.

9. Tell me every little detail of how you feel and what you are doing.
    I stared at it for a moment, thinking how it was so strange to see a yellow glow coming from a key. I leaned over and picked it up. It was shimmering in the light. When I held it in my hand, it started to play music, like from a music box. I slipped the key in my pocket and ran home as quickly as possible. When I got in my bedroom where no one was looking, I took the key out. I noticed it was old and had the same shape as the key hole in a secret door in my attic.

10. Now leave the reader hanging. Make them want to read more.
    I went up to the attic and pushed the key into the keyhole. It fit perfectly! The key shined brighter, and the music got louder! I turned the key slowly.

B Paragraph

It all started one ordinary Wednesday when I was walking home from school. I was listening to music on my iPhone, texting my best friend about soccer practice when I stumbled upon a glowing key in the middle of the sidewalk. I stared at it for a moment, thinking how it was so strange to see a yellow glow coming from a key. I leaned over and picked it up. It was shimmering in the light. When I held it in my hand, it started to play music, like music from a music box. I slipped the key in my pocket and ran home as quickly as possible. When I got in my bedroom where no one was looking, I took the key out. I noticed it was old and had the same shape as the keyhole in a secret door in my attic. I went up to the attic and pushed the key into the keyhole. It fit perfectly! The key shined brighter, and the music got louder! I turned the key slowly.

11. You want your B to be a long paragraph. NOT super long, but about 5-7 Lines. (Count the actual lines on the paper.)

12. Okay, let's move onto the T1 paragraph. This is about going inside the secret door.

    Example T1:
    As quick as a blink, the door opened. It was still dark, but I could hear the same music coming from inside. I stepped inside and started yelling, "Hello? Is anyone in here?" There was no answer. As I walked further inside, I could see a glowing yellow light in the distance. I figured if I kept walking, I would sooner or later get to the light. Then all of a sudden, I took one step and lost all my balance. I fell into some sort of colorful tunnel that kept winding me around and around until I was dizzy. I fell out of the sky and landed hard on the ground. When I woke up, I was in an underground world!

13. Now T2 is about being in the underground world.

    Example T2:

    Standing all around me were these little people, dressed in overalls, with colorful hair. They were wondering where I came from. I introduced myself and asked them where I was. They told me "Troll Land." I knew they were familiar to me but had no idea they actually were living creatures in their own world. The trolls explained that in order for me to get home, I would have to find the Treasure Chest of Troll Land. I would have to get the magic key out of the treasure chest to get back home. My parents would be looking for me if I was gone too long, so I felt determined to find that treasure chest. I searched high and low and found nothing. When I was sitting against a tree to take a short nap, I noticed a pink glow coming from a bush nearby. I ran toward it. Coincidentally, it was the treasure box!

14. Now T3 is all about getting the treasure chest. Remember, tell me every STEP and every DETAIL. Help to PAINT a picture in my head.

    Example T3:

    Immediately, I opened it with my magic key and grabbed the other magic key inside. This new magic key glowed pink and still played the same kind of music. I left the treasure box open on the ground and started running toward the area where I had fallen from the sky. I thanked the trolls for all their help and explained to them that I had to be home before dinner so that I wouldn't get in trouble with my parents. They were understanding, hugged me, and said goodbye. There, hanging, was a long ladder that reached past the clouds into the sky. I started climbing it.

15. Now your ending is about getting back home. Tell about your day, how you feel, and what you did when you got back.

    Example E:

    I kept climbing and climbing farther and farther into the sky until I reached past the clouds. I couldn't see Troll Land anymore, and I could sense that I was getting closer to the door that led me to Troll Land in the first place. Finally, the brown, wooden door that I had fallen into was only a few stairs away. I hurled myself up into the doorway and closed the door. I was once again in a totally black room. All of a sudden, I heard my mom say, "Wake up! It's time for dinner." When I opened my eyes, I was so confused. Had I really gone to Troll Land, or was I dreaming? When I got up to go downstairs, a key fell from my bed onto the floor. It was glowing pink and playing music.

16. Review completed essay with students.

Example Completed Essay

It all started one ordinary Wednesday when I was walking home from school. I was listening to music on my iPhone, texting my best friend about soccer practice when I stumbled upon a glowing key in the middle of the sidewalk. I stared at it for a moment, thinking how it was so strange to see a yellow glow coming from a key. I leaned over and picked it up. It was shimmering in the light. When I held it in my hand, it started to play music, like music from a music box. I slipped the key in my pocket and ran home as quickly as possible. When I got in my bedroom where no one was looking, I took the key out. I noticed it was old and had the same shape as the keyhole in a secret door in my attic. I went up to the attic and pushed the key into the keyhole. It fit perfectly! The key shined brighter, and the music got louder! I turned the key slowly.

As quick as a blink, the door opened. It was still dark, but I could hear the same music coming from inside. I stepped inside and started yelling, "Hello? Is anyone in here?" There was no answer. As I walked further inside, I could see a glowing yellow light in the distance. I figured if I kept walking, I would sooner or later get to the light. Then all of a sudden, I took one step and lost all my balance. I fell into some sort of colorful tunnel that kept winding me around and around until I was dizzy. I fell out of the sky and landed hard on the ground. When I woke up, I was in an underground world!

Standing all around me were these little people, dressed in overalls, with colorful hair. They were wondering where I came from. I introduced myself and asked them where I was. They told me "Troll Land." I knew they were familiar to me but had no idea they actually were living creatures in their own world. The trolls explained that in order for me to get home, I would have to find the Treasure Chest of Troll Land. I would have to get the magic key out of the treasure chest to get back home. My parents would be looking for me if I was gone too long, so I felt determined to find that treasure chest. I searched high and low and found nothing. When I was sitting against a tree to take a short nap, I noticed a pink glow coming from a bush nearby. I ran toward it. Coincidentally, it was the treasure box!

Immediately, I opened it with my magic key and grabbed the other magic key inside. This new magic key glowed pink and still played the same kind of music. I left the treasure box open on the ground and started running toward the area where I had fallen from the sky. I thanked the trolls for all their help and explained to them that I had to be home before dinner so that I wouldn't get in trouble with my parents. They were understanding, hugged me, and said goodbye. There, hanging, was a long ladder that reached past the clouds into the sky. I started climbing it.

I kept climbing and climbing farther and farther into the sky until I reached past the clouds. I couldn't see Troll Land anymore, and I could sense that I was getting closer to the door that led me to Troll Land in the first place. Finally, the brown, wooden door that I had fallen into was only a few stairs away. I hurled myself up into the doorway and closed the door. I was once again in a totally black room. All of a sudden, I heard my mom say, "Wake up! It's time for dinner." When I opened my eyes, I was so confused. Had I really gone to Troll Land, or was I dreaming? When I got up to go downstairs, a key fell from my bed onto the floor. It was glowing pink and playing music.

WRITING: LESSON 81

Today the students will be learning how to use transition words in a narrative essay.

1. Explain that for narrative essays, we do not use the transition words first, second, third, to begin with, etc. We have narrative transitions that we can use. They can be used for any paragraph, as long as it makes sense.

2. Pass out the list of "Narrative Transition Words."

3. Tell students that from now on, when they write a narrative essay, you expect them to use transition words.

4. Hand out "Example Essay" that shows where and how narrative transitions are used.

5. Put the "Example Essay" that shows the use of transition words under the document camera.

6. Point out where the transition words are used in a narrative essay.

7. Explain to students that transition words for narrative are only used at the beginning of T1, T2, T3, and E. We do not use a transition word for the "B" paragraph because we start that paragraph with a story starter.

8. Remind students that their E transition word has to be finally, later, or something that concludes the essay.

9. Pass out the "Practice/Homework" sheet for today and let students begin writing the essay.

10. Remind students that they must use transition words for T1, T2, T3, and E.

11. During this time, walk around the room and work one-on-one with those students who need additional help.

12. Allow students to finish what is not done in class as homework.

List of Narrative Transition Words   Name:_____

Narrative Transition Words

After

Afterward

As soon as

Before

Finally

Later

Now

Not long after

Until

When

While

One day

Minutes later

Meanwhile

Immediately

Soon

Then

Next

In the meantime

Example Essay – Narrative Transitions   Name:_____

It all started one ordinary Wednesday when I was walking home from school. I was listening to music on my iPhone, texting my best friend about soccer practice when I stumbled upon a glowing key in the middle of the sidewalk. I stared at it for a moment, thinking how it was so strange to see a yellow glow coming from a key. I leaned over and picked it up. It was shimmering in the light. When I held it in my hand, it started to play music, like music from a music box. I slipped the key in my pocket and ran home as quickly as possible. When I got in my bedroom where no one was looking, I took the key out. I noticed it was old and had the same shape as the keyhole in a secret door in my attic. I went up to the attic and pushed the key into the keyhole. It fit perfectly! The key shined brighter, and the music got louder! I turned the key slowly.

Next, as quick as a blink, the door opened. It was still dark, but I could hear the same music coming from inside. I stepped inside and started yelling, "Hello? Is anyone in here?" There was no answer. As I walked further inside, I could see a glowing yellow light in the distance. I figured if I kept walking, I would sooner or later get to the light. Then all of a sudden, I took one step and lost all my balance. I fell into some sort of colorful tunnel that kept winding me around and around until I was dizzy. I fell out of the sky and landed hard on the ground. When I woke up, I was in an underground world!

Then, standing all around me were these little people, dressed in overalls, with colorful hair. They were wondering where I came from. I introduced myself and asked them where I was. They told me "Troll Land." I knew they were familiar to me but had no idea they actually were living creatures in their own world. The trolls explained that in order for me to get home, I would have to find the Treasure Chest of Troll Land. I would have to get the magic key out of the treasure chest to get back home. My parents would be looking for me if I was gone too long, so I felt determined to find that treasure chest. I searched high and low and found nothing. When I was sitting against a tree to take a short nap, I noticed a pink glow coming from a bush nearby. I ran toward it. Coincidentally, it was the treasure box!

After, I immediately opened it with my magic key and grabbed the other magic key inside. This new magic key glowed pink and still played the same kind of music. I left the treasure box open on the ground and started running toward the area where I had fallen from the sky. I thanked the trolls for all their help and explained to them that I had to be home before dinner so that I wouldn't get in trouble with my parents. They were understanding, hugged me, and said goodbye. There, hanging, was a long ladder that reached past the clouds into the sky. I started climbing it.

In the end, I kept climbing and climbing farther and farther into the sky until I reached past the clouds. I couldn't see Troll Land anymore, and I could sense that I was getting closer to the door that led me to Troll Land in the first place. Finally, the brown, wooden door that I had fallen into was only a few stairs away. I hurled myself up into the doorway and closed the door. I was once again in a totally black room. All of a sudden, I heard my mom say, "Wake up! It's time for dinner." When I opened my eyes, I was so confused. Had I really gone to Troll Land, or was I dreaming? When I got up to go downstairs, a key fell from my bed onto the floor. It was glowing pink and playing music.

Practice/Homework   Name:_____

*People dream of discovering gold. Imagine one day while you were gardening, you dug up gold.
Now tell a story about what you did with the gold once you found it.*

B_____

T1_____

T2_____

T3_____

E_____

B

T1

T2

T3

_____

_____

_____

_____

_____

_____

_____

_____

E

_____

_____

_____

WRITING: LESSON 82

Today the students will be learning about the narrative checklist and how to use it when writing narrative essays.

1. Hand out "Narrative Checklist" to students.

2. Explain that this checklist lists everything that should be included in a narrative essay.

3. From now on when we practice writing narrative essays, you will be required to fill out this checklist.

4. The checklist will ensure that you have included everything that is required in a narrative essay.

5. Let's look over this checklist and make sure we understand everything.

6. At the beginning of every paragraph, it says "Indent." We will no longer be using paper that says B, T1, T2, T3, and E on it. You must now write paragraphs and indent at the beginning of each one.

7. Look at the "B" paragraph requirements:
    - Must indent.
    - Must start with a story starter (Ex. Wait until you hear about the best day of my life...).
    - Have to describe the setting (where you are at the beginning of the story).
    - The paragraph must tell how the whole day started and details about how it happened.

8. T1, T2, and T3 have all of the same requirements:
    - Must indent.
    - Must use a transition word at the beginning of each paragraph.
    - Have to write details about what you saw and did.
    - Have to tell about how you felt (excited, sad, scared, confused).
    - Write 6-8 lines.
    - Have to lead your reader into the next paragraph by moving on to the next thing.
    - Must have details.

9. Now the "E" paragraph:
    - Have to indent.
    - Have to tell how you got back, changed back, or something stopped working.
    - Tell what you did when you got home.
    - Tell how the whole story ended (Think of the end of a movie!).
    - There should be at least 5 lines.

10. Hand out "Homework."

Narrative Checklist   Name:_____

"B" Paragraph
Indent   _____
Starts with a story starter   _____
Describes the setting   _____
How it all started   _____

T1 Paragraph
Indent   _____
Transition Word   _____
Details about what you saw   _____
Details about what you did   _____
Feeling   _____
Moving on to the next thing   _____
At least 6-8 lines   _____
Details   _____

T2 Paragraph
Indent   _____
Transition Word   _____
Details about what you saw   _____
Details about what you did   _____
Feeling   _____
Moving on to the next thing   _____
At least 6-8 lines   _____
Details   _____

T3 Paragraph
Indent   _____
Transition Word   _____
Details about what you saw   _____
Details about what you did   _____
Feeling   _____
Moving on to the next thing   _____
At least 6-8 lines   _____
Details   _____

"E" Paragraph
Indent   _____
How you got back, changed back, or
    something stopped working   _____
What you did when you got back home   _____
Feeling about your day   _____
At least 5 lines   _____
How the story ended   _____

Homework   Name:_____

**Everyone has a favorite celebrity. Think of one celebrity that you would love to meet.
Write a story about the time you met your favorite celebrity.**

B_____

T1_____

T2_____

T3_____

E_____

WRITING: LESSON 83

*Today students will be learning about adding details to their narrative stories.
Details are VERY important in a narrative essay because the reader
must be able to paint a picture in their head.*

1. Details are very important when writing a narrative essay.
2. Let's start with a simple example:
   - Let's pretend we are writing about a day we found a magic wand.
   - (Write on board) – *I found a wand.*
   - This sentence tells our reader nothing. We cannot paint a picture in our head at all because there are no details. I know nothing about the wand.
   - Give more details. *I found a magic wand that glowed pink and shimmered in sparkles.*
   - Now we can paint a picture. If we close our eyes while reading that sentence, we can create a picture of a glowing pink wand that was covered in sparkles.
3. Now let's look at a non-example:
   - Remind students not to get DETAIL CRAZY! We do not want them to overdo it. Give students an example of what you do not want them to do: *I found a small, magic wand that was glowing florescent pink in the sunlight and light pink in the shade and it had sparkles all over it with pink rhinestones around the handle.*
4. Every time we write, we have to write details so that our reader can create a picture in their head.
5. This is especially important when you go somewhere, like Troll Land, or find an underground world. These are made up places, so you need to describe with details. This is also important if you find a magic pair of shoes or a key. We need to know what they look like, so we can paint a picture in our head.

6. Let's try a few more examples on the board:

   Example 1: (Write on the board:) *I found a magic rock in a box.*
   - Now have students create a better sentence with details and write the new sentence on the board.
   - Example 1 Sample Sentence:
       I found a gold pebble that was shining bright yellow in a silver, sparkly box.

   Example 2: (Write on the board:) *I saw lots of stuff in Troll Land.*
   - Now have students create a better sentence with details and write the new sentence on the board.
   - Example 2 Sample Sentence:
       There were small, funny-looking people with hair that was all shades of the rainbow.

7. Now students should have a good understanding of what we mean by adding details.
8. Hand out "Student Practice" worksheet.
   - Tell students to write details about each of the people, places, or things listed.
9. Hand out "Homework."
   - Remind students to use transition words and details in their story.

Student Practice   Name:_____

Adding Details

Look at the following people, places, and items. Write as many details as possible about each of them on the lines. The first one is done for you.

1. Candyland

    marshmallow bunnies, lollipop flowers, milk chocolate river, gingerbread king, cotton candy

    sheep, white chocolate ducks, twizzler snakes, gummy worms

    _____

2. Santa Claus

    _____

    _____

    _____

3. Underwater World

    _____

    _____

    _____

4. Magic Crown

    _____

    _____

    _____

5. Magic Shoes

    _____

    _____

    _____

Homework   Name:_____

Suppose one morning you went to the bus stop and found a puppy. Think about what you would do with it. Now tell a story about what you would do with the puppy.

B_____

T1_____

T2_____

T3_____

E_____

_____

_____

_____

_____

_____

_____

_____

_____

_____

_____

_____

_____

_____

_____

_____

_____

_____

_____

_____

_____

_____

_____

_____

WRITING: LESSON 84

Today the students will be learning about dialogue in a narrative essay.

1. Explain to students that dialogue is when you use quotation marks to tell the reader what a character is saying. There are two types of dialogue used in stories: direct and indirect.

   - Direct dialogue is speech using the character's exact words. For this, quotation marks are used.
     Example - **"May I buy a new pair of shoes?" Lisa asked her mom.**

   - Indirect dialogue is a second-hand report of something that was said or written, but NOT the exact words in their original form.
     Example – **Lisa asked her mom for a new pair of shoes.**

2. You use quotation marks to indicate the words that are spoken by the characters.

   Example:
   My mom said, **"Get in the car. We are going to the doctor!"**

3. Remember, you do not have to use quotations for everything a character says. You only do this when you want to tell your reader a direct quote from the character. When you want them to know EXACTLY what the character is saying. Or you could say this same sentence as: *My mom told us to get in the car because we were going to the doctor.* This is when you are just telling your reader what the character said (indirect quote).

4. Let's say you wanted to say that your dad told you to go to bed. You want to put it in a direct quote. How would you write it?

   - Do this as an example on the board:
     My dad yelled, "Go to bed!"

5. It is important to teach where the comma goes, where the quotation marks go, and to make sure the end of the sentence punctuation is inside the quotations. This should be taught often through examples and practice.

6. Do the following 2 examples on the board:

   - Let's say Mary told us to wake up. How would we write this as a direct quote?
     Mary said, "Wake up!" or "Wake up!" Mary said.

   - Let's say Sue told us to run really fast. How do we write this as a direct quote?
     Sue screamed, "Run really fast!"

7. Do a couple more examples to make sure the students have a true understanding of how to write quotations.

    Example 1: Let's say someone asked you what happened.
    Example 1 Answer: **"What happened?" he asked.**

    Example 2: Let's say a little girl shouted to go away.
    Example 2 Answer: **The little girl shouted, "Go away!"**

8. Hand out the "Student Practice" worksheet.

    Answers:
    1) Richard said, "I am going to the zoo."
    2) "I want to eat ice cream now!" Jake said.
    3) My mom shouted, "Sit down, or you will not have dessert today!"
    4) "What is that?" I asked myself quietly.
    5) "Can you clean your dishes please?" my mom asked.
    6) Joey whispered, "Who is that?"

9. Tell the students to practice writing these quotations correctly.

10. Tell them from now on you want to see them trying to use quotations in their stories.

Student Practice

Name:_____

Quotations

Read each sentence. Rewrite each sentence as a quotation.
Make sure you add the correct punctuation.

1. Richard said I am going to the zoo

_____

_____

2. I want to eat ice cream now Jake said

_____

_____

3. My mom shouted sit down, or you will not have dessert today

_____

_____

4. What is that I asked myself quietly

_____

_____

5. Can you clean your dishes please my mom asked

_____

_____

6. Joey whispered who is that

_____

_____

WRITING: LESSON 85

Today the students will be writing a narrative essay. This is your opportunity to see who understands narrative and who needs additional help.

1. Explain to students that they will have 90 minutes to write.
2. They can use 10-15 minutes for planning and the rest of the time for writing.
3. They will be writing a narrative essay and will be timed.
4. After 10-15 minutes, students are to stop planning and start writing the essay.
5. Remind students of the following: (You may keep the anchor charts of these notes up during the test.)

B Paragraph:
5-7 lines
- Story Starter
- Setting
- How it started
- Details about what happened

T1, T2, and T3
10-12 Lines
- Transition Word
- Details about what you saw
- Details about what you did
- Feeling
- Moving on to the next thing

"E" paragraph:
5-7 Lines
- Tell how you got back, changed back, or something stopped working
- What you did when you got back
- Feeling about your day
- How the story ended

6. Hand out the test.
7. Remind students of the time restriction.
8. Allow them to start planning.
9. After 10-15 minutes, tell students planning time is over, and they should start writing.
10. When students have 10 minutes left, give them a 10 minute warning.
11. After 90 minutes, have students put their pencils down.
12. Collect, grade, and record test scores.

Test   Name:_____

Sometimes a class gets to go on a field trip. Before you write, think about a time your class went somewhere together. Now write a story about the time your class went on a field trip.

B_____

T1_____

T2_____

T3_____

E_____

_____

_____

_____

_____

_____

_____

_____

_____

_____

_____

_____

_____

_____

_____

_____

_____

_____

_____

_____

_____

_____

_____

_____

_____

_____

_____

_____

_____

_____

_____

_____

_____

_____

_____

_____

_____

_____

_____

_____

_____

_____

_____

_____

_____

_____

WRITING: LESSON 86
Conference/Revision Day

- Today you will be having small conferences with students discussing their writing results from yesterday.

- For those students who did everything correctly, you can pair them up with a struggling student to help them rewrite their essay.

- Students do not need to rewrite their entire essays, they can just rewrite the parts they need to fix.

  o For example: Let's say a student only wrote 6 lines in their T1 paragraph. Give them another piece of lined paper and have them rewrite just their T1 paragraph and make it 10-12 lines. Have them bring it to you once they complete it and have it checked.

  o Another example: Let's say a student did not finish their essay. Send them to their seats to finish up the essay and bring it to you once they complete it.

- For students who have completed everything and time is still remaining, give them the "Practice Essay" assignment.

B
_____
_____
_____
_____

T1
_____
_____
_____
_____
_____
_____
_____
_____

T2
_____
_____
_____
_____
_____
_____
_____
_____

T3
_____
_____
_____
_____
_____
_____
_____
_____

E
_____
_____
_____

Practice Essay

Name:_____

Suppose that one morning you woke up and you were only five inches tall. Think about what it would be like to be only five inches tall. Now tell a story about your day as a five-inch tall person.

B_____

T1_____

T2_____

T3_____

E_____

_____

_____

_____

_____

_____

_____

_____

_____

_____

_____

_____

_____

_____

_____

_____

_____

_____

_____

_____

_____

_____

_____

_____

WRITING: LESSON 87

Today the students will be writing a narrative essay. This is your opportunity to see who understands narrative and who needs additional help. While the students are writing each day, you will pull small groups and work on their individual needs.

1. Explain to students that on the writing test they are only allowed 90 minutes to write.
2. They can use 10-15 minutes for planning and the rest for writing.
3. Over the next few days, they will be writing a narrative essay, and it will be timed.
4. After 10-15 minutes, students are to stop planning and start writing the essay.
5. Remind students of the following: (You may keep the anchor charts of these notes up during the test.)

B Paragraph:

5-7 lines
- Story Starter
- Setting
- How it started
- Details about what happened

T1, T2, and T3

10-12 Lines
- Transition Word
- Details about what you saw
- Details about what you did
- Feeling
- Moving on to the next thing

"E" paragraph:

5-7 Lines
- Tell how the whole story ended
- What you did at the end of the story
- Feeling about your day
- What you did at the end

6. Hand out tests.
7. Remind students of the time restriction.
8. Allow them to start writing.
9. After 10-15 minutes, tell students that planning time is over and they should start writing.
10. When students have 10 minutes left, give them a 10 minute warning.
11. After 90 minutes, have students put their pencils down.

During testing time, pull students who may need additional assistance.

12. Collect, grade, and record test scores.

Test

Name:_____

Date:_____

Imagine you had a time machine that would take you into the past.
Think of the time period you would go to see and what you would do in that time period.
Write a story about that day.

B_____

T1_____

T2_____

T3_____

E_____

_____

_____

_____

_____

_____

_____

_____

_____

_____

_____

_____

_____

_____

_____

_____

_____

_____

_____

_____

_____

_____

_____

_____

_____

_____

_____

_____

_____

_____

_____

_____

_____

_____

_____

_____

_____

_____

_____

_____

_____

_____

_____

WRITING: LESSON 88
Conference/Revision Day

- Today you will be having small conferences with students discussing their writing results from yesterday.

- For those students who did everything correctly, you can pair them up with a struggling student to help them rewrite their essay.

- Students do not need to rewrite their entire essays, they can just rewrite the parts they need to fix.

    o For example: Let's say a student only wrote 6 lines in their T1 paragraph. Give them another piece of lined paper and have them rewrite just their T1 paragraph and make it 10-12 lines. Have them bring it to you once they complete it and have it checked.

    o Another example: Let's say a student did not finish their essay. Send them to their seats to finish up the essay and bring it to you once they complete it.

- For students who have completed everything and time is still remaining, give them the "Practice Essay" assignment.

Practice Essay

Name:_____

Many children love to read books. Imagine you found a mysterious book in your school library. Now tell what happened when you opened that book.

B_____

T1_____

T2_____

T3_____

E_____

_____

_____

_____

_____

_____

_____

_____

_____

_____

_____

_____

_____

_____

_____

_____

_____

_____

_____

_____

_____

_____

_____

_____

_____

_____

_____

_____

_____

_____

_____

_____

_____

_____

_____

_____

_____

_____

_____

_____

_____

SECTION 6

Additional Activities and Strategies

WRITING: LESSON 89

Highlighter Activity

This lesson is a revision activity that can be completed with any essay students have written.

** Each student will need 5 different color highlighters for this activity.

1. Hand out highlighters.

2. Hand back essays with checklists (either informative or opinion)

3. Start with the Introduction paragraph.
    - Ask students to highlight their Hook in pink.
    - Ask students to highlight their 3 Reasons/Topics sentence in green.
    - Ask students to highlight their Closing Statement in blue.
    ***As they highlight each one, have them check it off on the checklist.
    ***If students don't have something, make sure they put an "X" next to it on the checklist. This way they know what they are missing.

4. Move on to middle paragraphs.
    - Ask students to highlight the T sentence in green.
    - Ask students to highlight the 3 sentences about A in pink.
    - Ask students to highlight the 3 sentences about B in yellow.
    - Ask students to highlight their Wrap-Up in blue.

5. Do this for T1/R1, T2/R2, and T3/R3.

6. Move to Conclusion paragraph.
    - Ask students to highlight their "Restate the Topic" sentence in pink.
    - Ask students to highlight their 3 Reasons/Topics sentence in green.
    - Ask students to highlight their Thought/Feeling in blue.

    These colors are just suggestions. The whole point is that students figure out what they are missing on their own. We want them to say, "But I don't have 3 sentences about A, I only have 2," so then you can tell them they always need to have 3.

7. Hand out blank lined paper.

8. Tell students they will be revising the paragraphs that they need to make changes to.

9. Students do NOT need to rewrite the whole essay, only the paragraphs they need to change.

Example Essay

How much do you really know about the 4th of July? On the 4th of July, we honor America's freedom, have extravagant celebrations, and do fun outdoor activities. People all across this country still celebrate July 4th because they feel blessed that America is a free country!

First, the 4th of July is remembered as the time when America cut ties with Great Britain because they were being treated unfairly and wanted freedom. According to History of the 4th of July, "They thought they were paying too much money in taxes." This made Americans upset! They also were angry because they didn't have voting rights. When America got its independence from Britain, the Declaration of Independence was written. As stated by History of the 4th of July, Thomas Jefferson and his team of men came together to sign it on July 4, 1776, which gave freedom to all Americans. This must have been a big, exciting day for the American people! That's why we acknowledge this day as a major holiday!

Second, on the 4th of July, many people hold extravagant celebrations. People celebrate by having parades says 4th of July Celebrations. This is a very fun event! Everyone lines the streets to watch the bands, floats, and entertainers go by. Some people in the parades even throw candy out to the spectators! Also, people hold ceremonies on the 4th of July. The author states in 4th of July Celebrations that "The city of Philadelphia holds a Historic Celebration of Freedom Ceremony." During this ceremony, people go to Independence Hall to listen to inspirational music, learn about American history, and recite the Declaration of Independence says the same text. This event brings Americans together to remember how lucky they are to live in a country that is free.

Third, July 4th is a time when many people do outdoor activities. Many people decorate their houses in red, white, and blue and have barbecues states the text 4th of July Celebrations. In the same text it says "Homes and businesses proudly fly the American flag" on this day. By doing this, people show that they are proud to be an American. Also, a tradition on the 4th of July is to go watch fireworks. Once it gets dark, many families go watch a colorful display of fireworks to end the holiday says the author of 4th of July Celebrations. This is the best part of the day because the fireworks are so beautiful! Fireworks are a great grand finale for a fantastic holiday!

As you can see, the 4th of July is a fun holiday to celebrate. On this day, people acknowledge America's freedom, they hold extravagant celebrations, and they plan fun outdoor activities. Every year on the 4th of July, we unite and remember how lucky we are to be living in a free country!

Informative Checklist   Name:_____

_____ 5 paragraphs

_____ Indent 5 times

I

_____ 3 sentences
_____ 1. Hook
_____ 2. 3 topics
_____ 3. Closing

T1

_____ Transition Word   _____ Quote
_____ T sentence   _____ Paraphrase
_____ 3-4 sentences about A   _____ Own thoughts/ideas
_____ 3-4 sentences about B
_____ W sentence
_____ 8-10 sentences
_____ 1-2 Reference Sources

T2

_____ Transition Word   _____ Quote
_____ T sentence   _____ Paraphrase
_____ 3-4 sentences about A   _____ Own thoughts/ideas
_____ 3-4 sentences about B
_____ W sentence
_____ 8-10 sentences
_____ 1-2 Reference Sources

T3

_____ Transition Word   _____ Quote
_____ T sentence   _____ Paraphrase
_____ 3-4 sentences about A   _____ Own thoughts/ideas
_____ 3-4 sentences about B
_____ W sentence
_____ 8-10 sentences
_____ 1-2 Reference Sources

C

_____ Give an overview (summary) of the topic
_____ Restate 3 topics
_____ Thought or feeling about the topic

Opinion Checklist   Name:_____

_____ 5 paragraphs

_____ Indent 5 times

I

_____ 3 sentences
_____ 1. Hook
_____ 2. 3 Reasons
_____ 3. Closing
_____ Clearly state opinion

R1

_____ Transition Word   _____ Quote
_____ T sentence   _____ Paraphrase
_____ 3-4 sentences about A   _____ Own thoughts/ideas
_____ 3-4 sentences about B
_____ W sentence
_____ State opinion
_____ 8-10 sentences
_____ 1-2 Reference Sources

R2

_____ Transition Word   _____ Quote
_____ T sentence   _____ Paraphrase
_____ 3-4 sentences about A   _____ Own thoughts/ideas
_____ 3-4 sentences about B
_____ W sentence
_____ State opinion
_____ 8-10 sentences
_____ 1-2 Reference Sources

R3

_____ Transition Word   _____ Quote
_____ T sentence   _____ Paraphrase
_____ 3-4 sentences about A   _____ Own thoughts/ideas
_____ 3-4 sentences about B
_____ W sentence
_____ State opinion
_____ 8-10 sentences
_____ 1-2 Reference Sources

C

_____ Give an overview (summary) of the topic – state opinion
_____ Restate 3 reasons
_____ Thought/Feeling about the topic

WRITING: LESSON 90

Race Against the Clock – Raffle Ticket Activity

The great thing about this lesson is that the students think this is a game, but we are actually getting a timed assessment out of them. Think of this as an assessment, but **FUN**!

> *The following passages will be used in today's lesson:*
>
> **Marvelous Magnets**
>
> **Uses of Magnets**

Prompt:

You have read several sources about magnets. Write an informative essay describing the uses of magnets and how they work. Use evidence from the sources to support your writing.

1. Tell students that today they will be playing "Race Against the Clock" with raffle tickets.

2. Write the prompt on the board.

3. Hand out the planning sheets and lined paper.

4. Tell students they will be given:
   20-30 min - Reading
   15 min - Planning
   10 min - Introduction paragraph
   15-20 min - T1/R1, T2/R2, T3/R3
   10 min - Conclusion paragraph

   Students will get a raffle ticket if they finish before time is up AND if it is written correctly.

5. Review prompt and tell students they will have 20-30 minutes to read the passages.

6. Once students are done reading the passages, tell them to put their pencils up in the air. Tell them they now have 15 minutes to plan. Say GO! Time students for 15 minutes. As they are working, walk around the room to check their planning. After 15 minutes, anyone who is finished and planned correctly receives a raffle ticket.

   (Continue to do this for each paragraph.)

7. Set the timer for 10 minutes, tell students to write the Introduction paragraph. Anyone who finishes in 10 minutes receives a raffle ticket.

8. Time T1 – 15-20 minutes- Anyone who finishes and writes it correctly, gets a ticket.

9. Time T2 – 15-20 minutes- Anyone who finishes and writes it correctly, gets a ticket.

10. Time T3 – 15-20 minutes- Anyone who finishes and writes it correctly, gets a ticket.

11. Set timer for 10 minutes, tell students to write the Conclusion. Anyone who finishes and writes it correctly in 10 minutes receives a raffle ticket.

12. Last 15 minutes of class, hand out raffle prizes.

Planning Sheet

_____

_____

_____

_____

_____

_____

_____

_____

_____

_____

_____

_____

_____

_____

_____

_____

_____

_____

WRITING: LESSON 91

You Write, They Write

**This can be used for informative and opinion writing.*

> *The following passages will be used in today's lesson:*
>
> **The Cave of the Crystals**
>
> **Cave of the Crystals: How Crystals Form**

1. Hand out lined paper and planning sheet.

2. Tell students that today you will both be writing an essay. You will be modeling first, and then they will write. This will be done for each paragraph. (Example prompt and essay is included with this lesson.)

3. Start with the teacher modeled planning. Watch the clock, and begin planning for this prompt. Students should not be writing anything during this time. They are watching and listening to you model how to plan for this prompt.

4. Think aloud as you plan and keep an eye on the clock. Make sure you spend no more than 15-20 minutes on planning.

5. Once you are done modeling how to plan, have students start to plan for the same prompt. Make sure you tell them NOT to steal any of your ideas. They need to come up with their own plan. As students are planning, walk around to see who is doing it correctly and conference with those who need additional assistance.

6. After 15-20 minutes, students should be done planning.

7. Model your "I" Paragraph. After you model, have students write their "I" Paragraph.
   - Make sure students are watching you as you write.
   - Think aloud, let them hear your thought process.
   - Once you have finished, let students write their "I" Paragraphs.
   - Walk around the room and check their paragraphs.
   - Have students put their pencils down after finishing their I.

8. Write your R1/T1. After you model have students write their R1/T1.
9. Continue to do this for the rest of essay. Follow this pattern of, "You write, They write." Take note of students who are still struggling and may need small group instruction.

10. As you walk around the room and read through the student essays, be sure to share good examples and non-examples with the class.

Prompt: Write an informative essay to present to your class about crystals and how they form. Use information from the passages in your essay.

Example Planning
I   Crystals
T1. Naica Mine   a. Cave of Crystals   b. Conditions
T2. Growth   a. Temperature   b. Fluid
T3. Visitors   a. What to Wear?   b. Safety
C.   Crystals

Example Essay:

    I'm sure you have seen a piece of jewelry with a crystal on it. Have you ever wondered where it came from? Crystals come from mines like the Naica Mine, these mines have the perfect conditions for crystals to grow, and they have plenty of visitors who come to see these large crystals. Crystals can be fascinating to learn about!

    To start off, crystals can be found in the Naica Mine. This mine has a place called the Cave of Crystals. According to The Cave of Crystals, the Naica Mine can be found in Chihueahuea, Mexico. Miners accidentally hammered into the cave and found the biggest crystals in the world! That must have been an incredible sight! "Some of them were 50 feet long" states the author of The Cave of Crystals. This cave has special conditions that are good for crystal growth. As many would think, the farther down into a cave, the cooler it would be. But this is not the case for the Naica mine, as it gets hotter when going deeper. This must be a part of the reason why crystals grow in this cave but not all caves. Therefore, miners and visitors must be careful when going into the mine to see the crystals.

    To continue, these crystals have the perfect growing conditions in the Naica Mine. The reason why these crystals grow so big is because of the hot temperature. "Today, there is still a magma chamber about three miles below the cave" which causes the cave to be very hot says, Cave of Crystals: How Crystals Form. That's why these crystals grow from the walls, ceiling, and even the floor. Also, hot fluids from the magma below travel up to the mine, and they carry minerals that form the crystals says Cave of Crystals: How Crystals Form. These minerals are key to crystal formation and growth! They get larger the longer they stay under the hot fluids. This is why crystals form so large in the Naica Mine.

    Lastly, many visitors come to visit the Naica Mine and its crystals. The article The Cave of Crystals says that "Before people enter the cave, they must put on gloves and boots." They also must wear protective masks that blow cool air. If they don't wear these masks, they may struggle to breathe down in the mine. Visitors must take precaution, as they could possibly suffer from heatstroke. They must use the lamps on top of their masks to help guide them through the dark mine. According to The Cave of Crystals, they cannot stay in the mine any longer than 20 minutes, as it is too hot for the body to withstand it! Although this can be a dangerous trip, it seems it is worth it to see the world's largest crystals!

    In conclusion, it's very interesting learning how crystals are formed! Crystals come from mines such as the Naica Mine, these mines have the perfect conditions for crystals to grow, and they have plenty of visitors who come to see these large crystals. It would be so incredibly breathtaking to see this crystal cave!

WRITING: LESSON 92

Fancy Transitions

***Informative and Opinion Writing*

In this lesson, you will be teaching students about fancy transition words. They have learned some basic transition words in the lessons so far, but now that they understand the structure of the essay, we want them to be able to use higher-level words that transition smoothly from paragraph to paragraph.

1. Explain to students that we want them to be able to use higher-level words that transition smoothly from paragraph to paragraph.

2. Show an example essay that has basic transition words.

3. Now show the list of fancy transition words. Then show the example essay that uses the fancy transition words. Read aloud and show students how these transition words make it easier to flow from one paragraph to the next.

4. Put the list of fancy transitions back under the document camera.

5. Tell students to pick 5-6 fancy transition words that they want to use and write them on an index card like this:

My Fancy Transition Words - - - - -

6. Explain to students that they can use these when writing an informative or opinion essay.

7. Have students tape these cards to their desks and/or put them in the front of their writing folder.

8. Hand out "Homework Essay."

***Teachers – make an anchor chart of these words after the lesson**

Example Essay

Name:_____

Basic Transition Words

I'm sure you have seen a piece of jewelry with a crystal on it. Have you ever wondered where it came from? Crystals come from mines like the Naica Mine, these mines have the perfect conditions for crystals to grow, and they have plenty of visitors who come to see these large crystals. Crystals can be fascinating to learn about!

To start off, crystals can be found in the Naica Mine. This mine has a place called the Cave of Crystals. According to <u>The Cave of Crystals</u>, the Naica Mine can be found in Chihueahuea, Mexico. Miners accidentally hammered into the cave to find the biggest crystals in the world! That must have been an incredible sight! "Some of them were 50 feet long" states the author of <u>The Cave of Crystals</u>. This cave has special conditions that are good for crystal growth. As many would think, the farther down into a cave, the cooler it would be. But this is not the case for the Naica mine, as it gets hotter when going deeper. This must be a part of the reason why crystals grow in this cave and not all caves. Therefore, miners and visitors must be careful when going into the mine to see the crystals.

To continue, these crystals have the perfect growing conditions in the Naica Mine. The reason why these crystals grow so big is because of the hot temperature. "Today, there is still a magma chamber about three miles below the cave" which causes the cave to be very hot says, <u>Cave of Crystals: How Crystals Form</u>. That's why these crystals grow from the walls, ceiling, and even the floor. Also, hot fluids from the magma below travel up to the mine, and they carry minerals that form the crystals says <u>Cave of Crystals: How Crystals Form</u>. These minerals are key to crystal formation and growth! They get larger the longer they stay under the hot fluids. This is why crystals form so large in the Naica Mine.

Lastly, many visitors come to visit the Naica Mine and its crystals. The article <u>The Cave of Crystals</u> says that "Before people enter the cave, they must put on gloves and boots." They also must wear protective masks that blow cool air. If they don't wear these masks, they may struggle to breathe down in the mine. Visitors must take precaution, as they could possibly suffer from heatstroke. They must use the lamps on top of their masks to help guide them through the dark mine. According to <u>The Cave of Crystals</u>, they cannot stay in the mine any longer than 20 minutes, as it is too hot for the body to withstand it! Although this can be a dangerous trip, it seems it is worth it to see the world's largest crystals!

In conclusion, it's very interesting learning how crystals are formed! Crystals come from mines like the Naica Mine, these mines have the perfect conditions for crystals to grow, and they have plenty of visitors who come to see these large crystals. It would be so incredibly breathtaking to see this crystal cave!

Transition Word List   Name:_____

Fancy **Transition Words**

<u>R1, R2, and R3</u>

As can be expected
Clearly
Obviously
Of course
By the same token
Comparatively
In comparison
In the same way
Moreover
As far as
Furthermore
In contrast
Not only
Likewise

In support of this
The next point
As well as
From my point of view
In the first place
On one hand
On the other hand
Even though
Obviously
As a matter of fact
Not to mention
An interesting fact is
It is important to note that
One example that stands out is

<u>Conclusion</u>

For the reasons above
As you can see
As I have noted
Without a doubt
In short
In any case
In other words
In summation
As discussed earlier

Example Essay   Name:_____

Fancy Transition Words

I'm sure you have seen a piece of jewelry with a crystal on it. Have you ever wondered where it came from? Crystals come from mines like the Naica Mine, these mines have the perfect conditions for crystals to grow, and they have plenty of visitors who come to see these large crystals. Crystals can be fascinating to learn about!

An interesting fact is crystals can be found in the Naica Mine. This mine has a place called the Cave of Crystals. According to The Cave of Crystals, the Naica Mine can be found in Chihueahuea, Mexico. Miners accidentally hammered into the cave and found the biggest crystals in the world! That must have been an incredible sight! "Some of them were 50 feet long" states the author of The Cave of Crystals. This cave has special conditions that are good for crystal growth. As many would think, the farther down into a cave, the cooler it would be. But this is not the case for the Naica mine, as it gets hotter when going deeper. This must be a part of the reason why crystals grow in this cave and not all caves. Therefore, miners and visitors must be careful when going into the mine to see the crystals.

By the same token, these crystals have the perfect growing conditions in the Naica Mine. The reason why these crystals grow so big is because of the hot temperature. "Today, there is still a magma chamber about three miles below the cave" which causes the cave to be very hot says, Cave of Crystals: How Crystals Form. That's why these crystals grow from the walls, ceiling, and even the floor. Also, hot fluids from the magma below travel up to the mine, and they carry minerals that form the crystals says Cave of Crystals: How Crystals Form. These minerals are key to crystal formation and growth! They get larger the longer they stay under the hot fluids. This is why crystals form so large in the Naica Mine.

It is important to note that many visitors come to visit the Naica Mine and its crystals. The article The Cave of Crystals says that "Before people enter the cave, they must put on gloves and boots." They also must wear protective masks that blow cool air. If they don't wear these masks, they may struggle to breathe down in the mine. Visitors must take precaution, as they could possibly suffer from heatstroke. They must use the lamps on top of their masks to help guide them through the dark mine. According to The Cave of Crystals, they cannot stay in the mine any longer than 20 minutes, as it is too hot for the body to withstand it! Although this can be a dangerous trip, it seems it is worth it to see the world's largest crystals!

In summation, it's very interesting learning how crystals are formed! Crystals come from mines like the Naica Mine, these mines have the perfect conditions for crystals to grow, and they have plenty of visitors who come to see these large crystals. It would be so incredibly breathtaking to see this crystal cave!

Homework Essay   Name:_____

> *The following passages will be used in today's lesson:*
>
> **King Cobra**
>
> **Nile Crocodile**
>
> **Chameleons**

Prompt:

You have read several sources about reptiles. Write an informative essay about reptiles. Use evidence from the text to support your response.

Reminder: Use your Fancy transition words.

I _____

T1_____   a. _____

                                        b. _____

T2_____   a. _____

                                        b. _____

T3_____   a. _____

                                        b. _____

C _____

_____

_____

_____

_____

_____

_____

_____

_____

_____

_____

_____

_____

_____

_____

_____

_____

_____

_____

_____

_____

_____

_____

_____

_____

WRITING: LESSON 93
Opinion Writing Vocabulary

In this lesson you will be teaching students vocabulary words to use in their opinion essays.

The following passages will be used in today's lesson:

Stop Junk Food in Schools
Keep the Treats in School

Prompt:

You have read several sources about the importance of children eating junk food. Write an essay stating your opinion on whether or not school cafeterias should be allowed to sell junk food. Support your answer with evidence from the text.

1. Explain to students that although the structure of an informative and opinion essay is the same, it is important to differentiate the two by the language and vocabulary you use in your writing. Throughout your opinion essays, you want to make sure you are clearly showing your feeling/thoughts about the topic.

2. Show the list of "Opinion Vocabulary." Explain to students that these are examples of words and phrases you want to make sure you are using in your opinion essays. These words show your reader how you feel and what you think about the topic. This is important because the main point of the essay is to tell your opinion. You should not just simply be giving information - that is an informative essay.

3. Hand out "Opinion Vocabulary" list to all students.

4. Today you will be writing part of an essay together and using these opinion vocabulary words throughout the essay.

5. Hand out the articles on junk food to students. Review the prompt.

6. Read the articles on junk food.

7. As a class, plan for the prompt.

8. Together, start writing the essay. Ask students for ideas and what to write for each paragraph.

9. Throughout the essay, make sure you refer to the "Opinion Vocabulary" list and use those words and phrases. As you use them, highlight them to emphasize where they are and how they are used.

10. After writing I, R1, and R2 let students finish the rest on their own. Remind students that they MUST use words from the "Opinion Vocabulary" list in their essay. Tell students to highlight the words/phrases whenever they use them in the essay.

Opinion Vocabulary   Name:_____

Opinion Writing – Vocabulary

In my opinion

It seems to me that

My personal view is that

In my experience

As far as I can see

From what I know

I believe

I think

That is why I think

I am sure

I am certain

Personally, I think/feel

I am convinced

It is clear that

As far as I'm concerned

I'd like to point out that

If you ask me

What I think is

In my view

Homework Essay   Name:_____

> *The following passages will be used in today's lesson:*
>
> **Stop Junk Food in Schools**
> **Keep the Treats in School**

Prompt:

You have read several sources about the importance of children eating junk food. Write an essay stating your opinion on whether or not school cafeterias should be allowed to sell junk food. Support your answer with evidence from the text.

Reminder: Use words from the "Opinion Vocabulary" list.

I _____

R1 _____   a. _____

                                           b. _____

R2 _____   a. _____

                                           b. _____

R3 _____   a. _____

                                           b. _____

C _____

_____

_____

_____

_____

_____

_____

_____

_____

_____

_____

_____

_____

_____

_____

_____

_____

_____

_____

_____

_____

_____

_____

WRITING: LESSON 94
Text Evidence – Ways to Show Evidence

In this lesson you will be teaching students new and different ways to show evidence from the text.

The following passages will be used in today's lesson:

How Fossils Form
Where to Look for Fossils
The Ages of the Dinosaurs

Prompt:

You have read several sources about fossils. Write an informative essay explaining how fossils are formed. Use evidence from the text to support your answer.

1. Explain to students that in previous lessons they learned how to use Evidence-Based Terminology. This is how we show that we got the information from the text. Some examples are: "According to the author..." "In paragraph two it states..." or "The author says..."

2. In today's lesson, we will be going over different ways to show evidence from the text. This is very important when writing an informative or an opinion essay. The state writing assessment requires support to be evidence-based, so you must show this through the use of Evidence-Based Terminology.

3. Review rule when writing informative and opinion essays:
    You must reference your sources at least 1-2 times per middle paragraph.
    Try not to use the same word/phrase more than once in the entire essay.

4. Review the different ways they can reference their sources in an essay (see next page).

5. Tell students that today they will be writing an essay and using some of the new ways to reference their sources. Each time they reference their sources have them highlight or circle the word/phrase.

6. Hand out "Student Practice" worksheet.

7. As students write, share examples and non-examples under the document camera.

Different ways to Reference your Sources

State the title
Ex. In the text <u>Alligators at Risk</u>, it states...

State the author
Ex. In the text by Jon Smith it states...

State the source number (if listed)
Ex. According to Source 3...

State the page number and paragraph number
Ex. On page 6, paragraph 3 it says that...

☆ Students can also reference their source in the beginning of the sentence using EBT or at the end of the sentence using parentheses.

Ex. In the text by Jon Smith it states that alligators live in many different habitats. ← States the author's name in the beginning of the sentence using EBT

OR

Ex. Alligators live in many different habitats (Jon Smith). ← States the author's name at the end of the sentence in parenthesis

Evidence Based Terminology

According to the author

The author states

The author says

In the passage, the author says/states

On page 5

According to the text

In paragraph 2

Based on information from the text

The author writes that

According to page 2 of the passage

From the reading I know

Student Practice   Name:_____

> *The following passages will be used in today's lesson:*
>
> **How Fossils Form**
> **Where to Look for Fossils**
> **The Ages of the Dinosaurs**

Prompt:

You have read several sources about fossils. Write an informative essay explaining how fossils are formed. Use evidence from the text to support your answer.

I _____

T1_____   a. _____

                                            b. _____

T2_____   a. _____

                                            b. _____

T3_____   a. _____

                                            b. _____

C _____

_____

_____

_____

_____

_____

_____

_____

_____

_____

_____

_____

_____

_____

_____

_____

_____

_____

_____

_____

_____

_____

_____

_____

_____

_____

_____

_____

_____

_____

_____

_____

_____

_____

_____

_____

_____

_____

_____

_____

_____

_____

_____

_____

WRITING: LESSON 95
Fast Planning Practice

**For today's lesson, you will need passages that were used in previous lessons.
This lesson may be completed over two days if needed.

1. Choose 10 sets of **reading passages and prompts** from previous lessons (informative and opinion).

2. Hand out one set at a time with a planning sheet.

3. Give students 15-20 minutes to read the passages (depending on text level and length).

4. Once everyone has completed reading the passages, start the timer and tell them they will have 10 -15 minutes to plan for the prompt.

5. After 15 minutes, tell students to put their pencils down. Take 2-3 minutes to let them share their 3 topics and As and Bs. Review examples and non-examples.

6. Then hand out the next set of passages and prompt. Give students 15-20 minutes to read the passages (depending on text level and length). Once everyone has completed reading the passages, start the timer and tell them they will have 10-15 minutes to plan for the prompt.

7. Complete this same process over and over until all 10 sets of passages and prompts are completed.

Example Text Sets and Prompts

Passages:
Florida Today: The Sunshine State
Florida's Farming
Prompt: **Write to inform your reader about farming.**

Passages:
Fossils and Insects – Amber
Fossils and Insects – Impressions
Fossils and Insects – Compressions
Prompt: **The readings talked about fossils and insects. Think about what you have learned from these articles. Write to inform your reader about fossils and insects.**

Passages:
Servicemen to Our Country
Code Talkers
Prompt: **The readings talked about important men in history. Think about what you have learned. Now write to inform your reader about these important groups of men in history.**

Passages:
History of Egypt
Visit Egypt!
Prompt: **The readings talked about Egypt. Think about what you have learned from these articles. Now write to inform your reader about Egypt.**

Passages:
All About Mountains
How Are Mountains Formed?
Fun in the Mountains
Appalachian Mountains
Prompt: **The readings talked about mountains. Think about what you have learned from these articles. Now write to inform your reader about mountains.**

Passages:
Let Us Chew Gum in School
No Gum in School!
Prompt: **The readings talked about chewing gum in school. Write an essay in which you give your opinion: Should students be allowed to chew gum in school? Use the information from the passages in your essay.**

Passages:
Recycling Paper Gives Schools Benefits
Recycling Helps to Reduce Pollution
Recycling Is Dirty
Recycling in Schools Benefits Communities
Prompt: **The readings talked about recycling. Think about what you have learned about recycling. Now write your opinion on whether or not schools should recycle.**

Passages:
Music Programs in Schools
Music Programs in School Are a Waste of Time
Prompt: **The readings talked about music programs in schools. Think about what you have learned. Write your opinion on whether or not music programs are important in schools.**

Passages:
A Growing Language
Learning Early
No Classes Needed
Prompt: **The readings talked about children learning a second language. Think about what you have learned from the articles. Now write your opinion on whether or not children should be required to learn a second language.**

Passages:
Allowance for Kids? No Way!
Kids Deserve an Allowance
Prompt: **The readings talked about giving kids an allowance. Think about what you have learned from these articles. Now write your opinion on whether or not you think kids deserve an allowance.**

Planning Sheet   Name:_____

Use this sheet to plan what you will write. The writing on this sheet will **NOT** be scored.

_____

_____

_____

_____

_____

_____

_____

_____

_____

_____

_____

_____

_____

_____

_____

_____

_____

_____

WRITING: LESSON 96

Opinion Writing Practice

Today the students will be writing an opinion essay.

The following passages will be used in today's lesson:

Making the Best Decision

Cats and Dogs

What Makes a Good Pet?

Prompt:

All families like to have a pet. You have read several sources about pets. Write an essay stating your opinion on what animal you feel is best as a pet. Use evidence from the sources to support your answer.

Ideas on how to use the text for today's lesson:

- **Test** – Time students for 120 minutes.

- **You Write, They Write** – Refer to Lesson 91.

- **Check Their Writing** – Have students start with planning. Once they are done, they have to raise their hand to have it checked by the teacher. Once it is checked, they can move on to the first paragraph. After writing the first paragraph, they have to raise their hand to have it checked by the teacher. Students continue this throughout the whole essay. This way they are getting each paragraph checked before moving on to the next.

- **Highlighter Activity** – As they write, have students highlight the different parts of their paragraphs.
  Introduction – Highlight Hook, 3-Reasons sentence, and Closing sentence in different colors.
  Middle – Highlight T, 3A, 3B, and W in different colors.
  Conclusion – Highlight Summary sentence, 3-Reasons, and Ending sentence in different colors.

- **Writing Around the Room** – Set up 5 tables or writing areas in the room. Label the areas as: Introduction, R1 paragraph, R2 paragraph, R3 paragraph, and Conclusion. Have students start in their seats with reading the text and planning. Once they are done planning, they will go to the area in the room labeled "Introduction" and write their Introduction paragraph. Once they are finished with their Introduction paragraph, they will go to the area in the room labeled "R1 paragraph" and write their R1 paragraph. Students will continue moving around the room until their essay is completed.

Planning Sheet   Name:_____

Use this sheet to plan what you will write. The writing on this sheet will **NOT** be scored.

_____

_____

_____

_____

_____

_____

_____

_____

_____

_____

_____

_____

_____

_____

_____

_____

_____

_____

_____

_____

_____

_____

_____

_____

_____

_____

_____

_____

_____

_____

_____

_____

_____

_____

_____

_____

_____

_____

_____

Go On

_____

_____

_____

_____

_____

_____

_____

_____

_____

_____

_____

_____

_____

_____

_____

_____

_____

_____

_____

Go On

WRITING: LESSON 97
Informative Writing Practice

Today the students will be writing an informative essay.

> *The following passages will be used in today's lesson:*
>
> **Bird Beaks**
>
> **Migrating Birds**
>
> **Bird Talk**

Prompt:
You have read several sources about birds. Write an informative essay to explain about birds. Use evidence from the text to support your answer.

Ideas on how to use the text for today's lesson:

- **Test** – Time students for 120 minutes.

- **You Write, They Write** – Refer to Lesson 91.

- **Check Their Writing** – Have students start with planning. Once they are done, they have to raise their hand to have it checked by the teacher. Once it is checked, they can move on to the first paragraph. After writing the first paragraph, they have to raise their hand to have it checked by the teacher. Students continue this throughout the whole essay. This way they are getting each paragraph checked before moving on to the next.

- **Highlighter Activity** – As they write, have students highlight the different parts of their paragraphs.
  Introduction – Highlight Hook, 3-Topics sentence, and Closing sentence in different colors.
  Middle – Highlight T, 3A, 3B, and W in different colors.
  Conclusion – Highlight Summary sentence, 3-Topics, and Ending sentence in different colors.

- **Writing Around the Room** – Set up 5 tables or writing areas in the room. Label the areas as: Introduction, T1 paragraph, T2 paragraph, T3 paragraph, and Conclusion. Have students start in their seats with reading the text and planning. Once they are done planning, they will go to the area in the room labeled "Introduction" and write their Introduction paragraph. Once they are finished with their Introduction paragraph, they will go to the area in the room labeled "T1 paragraph" and write their T1 paragraph. Students will continue moving around the room until their essay is completed.

Planning Sheet

Name:_____

Use this sheet to plan what you will write. The writing on this sheet will **NOT** be scored.

_____

_____

_____

_____

_____

_____

_____

_____

_____

_____

_____

_____

_____

_____

_____

_____

_____

_____

_____

_____

_____

_____

_____

_____

_____

_____

_____

_____

_____

_____

_____

_____

_____

_____

_____

_____

_____

_____

_____

_____

Go On ⟶

_____

_____

_____

_____

_____

_____

_____

_____

_____

_____

_____

_____

_____

_____

_____

_____

_____

_____

_____

_____

_____

_____

_____

Go On

WRITING: LESSON 98
Opinion Writing Practice

Today the students will be writing an opinion essay.

> *The following passages will be used in today's lesson:*
>
> **Parents in Favor of School Uniforms**
> **Why School Uniforms Are Good for Students**
> **Say Yes to Uniforms**
> **Uniform Rage**

Prompt:
The articles talked about students wearing a school uniform. Write an essay stating your opinion about whether or not students should have to wear uniforms to school. Support your opinion with evidence from the sources.

Ideas on how to use the text for today's lesson:

- **Test** – Time students for 120 minutes.

- **You Write, They Write** – Refer to Lesson 91.

- **Check Their Writing** – Have students start with planning. Once they are done, they have to raise their hand to have it checked by the teacher. Once it is checked, they can move on to the first paragraph. After writing the first paragraph, they have to raise their hand to have it checked by the teacher. Students continue this throughout the whole essay. This way they are getting each paragraph checked before moving on to the next.

- **Highlighter Activity** – As they write, have students highlight the different parts of their paragraphs.
  Introduction – Highlight Hook, 3-Reasons sentence, and Closing sentence in different colors.
  Middle – Highlight T, 3A, 3B, and W in different colors.
  Conclusion – Highlight Summary sentence, 3-Reasons, and Ending sentence in different colors.

- **Writing Around the Room** – Set up 5 tables or writing areas in the room. Label the areas as: Introduction, R1 paragraph, R2 paragraph, R3 paragraph, and Conclusion. Have students start in their seats with reading the text and planning. Once they are done planning, they will go to the area in the room labeled "Introduction" and write their Introduction paragraph. Once they are finished with their Introduction paragraph, they will go to the area in the room labeled "R1 paragraph" and write their R1 paragraph. Students will continue moving around the room until their essay is completed.

Planning Sheet

Name:_____

Use this sheet to plan what you will write. The writing on this sheet will **NOT** be scored.

_____

_____

_____

_____

_____

_____

_____

_____

_____

_____

_____

_____

_____

_____

_____

_____

_____

_____

_____

_____

_____

_____

_____

_____

_____

_____

_____

_____

_____

_____

_____

_____

_____

_____

_____

_____

_____

_____

_____

_____

Go On ⟹

_____

_____

_____

_____

_____

_____

_____

_____

_____

_____

_____

_____

_____

_____

_____

_____

_____

_____

_____

_____

_____

Go On ⟶

_____

_____

_____

_____

_____

_____

_____

_____

_____

_____

_____

_____

_____

_____

_____

_____

_____

_____

_____

_____

_____

_____

_____

WRITING: LESSON 99
Informative Writing Practice

Today the students will be writing an informative essay.

> *The following passages will be used in today's lesson:*
>
> **Ladybugs**
>
> **Honeybees**

Prompt:
You have just read passages about insects. Write an informative essay on how these insects are similar. Use details from the passages to support your answer.

Ideas on how to use the text for today's lesson:

- **Test** – Time students for 120 minutes.

- **You Write, They Write** – Refer to Lesson 91.

- **Check Their Writing** – Have students start with planning. Once they are done, they have to raise their hand to have it checked by the teacher. Once it is checked, they can move on to the first paragraph. After writing the first paragraph, they have to raise their hand to have it checked by the teacher. Students continue this throughout the whole essay. This way they are getting each paragraph checked before moving on to the next.

- **Highlighter Activity** – As they write, have students highlight the different parts of their paragraphs.
  Introduction – Highlight Hook, 3-Topics sentence, and Closing sentence in different colors.
  Middle – Highlight T, 3A, 3B, and W in different colors.
  Conclusion – Highlight Summary sentence, 3-Topics, and Ending sentence in different colors.

- **Writing Around the Room** – Set up 5 tables or writing areas in the room. Label the areas as: Introduction, T1 paragraph, T2 paragraph, T3 paragraph, and Conclusion. Have students start in their seats with reading the text and planning. Once they are done planning, they will go to the area in the room labeled "Introduction" and write their Introduction paragraph. Once they are finished with their Introduction paragraph, they will go to the area in the room labeled "T1 paragraph" and write their T1 paragraph. Students will continue moving around the room until their essay is completed.

Planning Sheet

Name:_____

Use this sheet to plan what you will write. The writing on this sheet will **NOT** be scored.

_____

_____

_____

_____

_____

_____

_____

_____

_____

_____

_____

_____

_____

_____

_____

_____

_____

_____

_____

_____

_____

_____

_____

_____

_____

_____

_____

_____

_____

_____

_____

_____

_____

_____

_____

_____

_____

_____

Go On ⟶

_____

_____

_____

_____

_____

_____

_____

_____

_____

_____

_____

_____

_____

_____

_____

_____

_____

_____

_____

_____

_____

_____

_____

Go On

_____

_____

_____

_____

_____

_____

_____

_____

_____

_____

_____

_____

_____

_____

_____

_____

_____

_____

_____

_____

_____

WRITING: LESSON 100
Opinion Writing Practice

Today the students will be writing an opinion essay.

The following passages will be used in today's lesson:

Recess to Success
Kids Need Recess
Education vs. Recess
Legal Liability

Prompt:
You have read several sources about giving students recess. Write an essay where you state your opinion on whether or not schools should provide recess time to students. Support your opinion with evidence from the sources.

Ideas on how to use the text for today's lesson:

- **Test** – Time students for 120 minutes.

- **You Write, They Write** – Refer to Lesson 91.

- **Check Their Writing** – Have students start with planning. Once they are done, they have to raise their hand to have it checked by the teacher. Once it is checked, they can move on to the first paragraph. After writing the first paragraph, they have to raise their hand to have it checked by the teacher. Students continue this throughout the whole essay. This way they are getting each paragraph checked before moving on to the next.

- **Highlighter Activity** – As they write, have students highlight the different parts of their paragraphs.
  Introduction – Highlight Hook, 3-Reasons sentence, and Closing sentence in different colors.
  Middle – Highlight T, 3A, 3B, and W in different colors.
  Conclusion – Highlight Summary sentence, 3-Reasons, and Ending sentence in different colors.

- **Writing Around the Room** – Set up 5 tables or writing areas in the room. Label the areas as: Introduction, R1 paragraph, R2 paragraph, R3 paragraph, and Conclusion. Have students start in their seats with reading the text and planning. Once they are done planning, they will go to the area in the room labeled "Introduction" and write their Introduction paragraph. Once they are finished with their Introduction paragraph, they will go to the area in the room labeled "R1 paragraph" and write their R1 paragraph. Students will continue moving around the room until their essay is completed.

Planning Sheet   Name:_____

Use this sheet to plan what you will write. The writing on this sheet will **NOT** be scored.

_____

_____

_____

_____

_____

_____

_____

_____

_____

_____

_____

_____

_____

_____

_____

_____

_____

_____

_____

_____

_____

_____

_____

_____

_____

_____

_____

_____

_____

_____

_____

_____

_____

_____

_____

_____

_____

_____

_____

Go On ⟹

_____

_____

_____

_____

_____

_____

_____

_____

_____

_____

_____

_____

_____

_____

_____

_____

_____

_____

_____

_____

Go On ⟹